The Pennsylvania Reader

By Trinka Hakes Noble

Illustrated by K. L. Darnell

Sleeping Bear Press™

310 North Main Street, Suite 300
Chelsea, MI 48118
www.sleepingbearpress.com

© 2007 Sleeping Bear Press is an imprint of The Gale Group, Inc.

Printed and bound in China.

10 9 8 7 6 5 4 3 2 1

Library of Congress Cataloging-in-Publication Data

Noble, Trinka Hakes.
The Pennsylvania reader / written by Trinka Hakes Noble ; illustrated
by K. L. Darnell.
p. cm. — (State reader series)
Summary: "Modeled after traditional primers, this book includes
individual stories, riddles, and poems about Pennsylvania's history,
famous people, and state symbols"—Provided by publisher.
ISBN: 978-1-58536-320-9
1. Pennsylvania—Literary collections. 2. Pennsylvania—Juvenile
literature. 3. Readers (Primary) I. Darnell, Kathryn, ill. II. Title.
PS3564.O265P46 2007
810.8'09748—dc22   2007015351

Preface

Pennsylvania has long been a place of reading and learning. William Penn, who founded the colony in 1681, strongly believed in educating the young. Early on, Quaker schools were established for colonial boys and girls. Many famous Pennsylvanians, like Betsy Ross and Daniel Boone, attended Quaker schools when they were young.

Another famous Pennsylvanian, Benjamin Franklin, added to this legacy of learning by founding the first free lending library. For many years, he also wrote and published a small booklet called *Poor Richard's Almanac.* All colonists loved *Poor Richard's Almanac* because it was filled with riddles, humor, popular sayings, drawings, poems, and useful information which made learning to read enjoyable and fun.

I hope you find *The Pennsylvania Reader* fun to read, too. This small book is patterned after early primers which taught children to read long ago. It is filled with poems, riddles, drawings, fictional letters and stories, hidden pictures, and even a play and history timeline, too. There

is something to interest every reader, young and old.
I hope you enjoy reading and learning about the culture,
history, and symbols of Pennsylvania and that you share
this small book with family, friends, and classmates.

Your friend,
Trinka Hakes Noble

For all the children of Pennsylvania.

T.H.N.

For my mom, Jean Darnell—
Her childhood in Pennsylvania (and the stories!)
is my claim to Pennsylvania roots.
Thanks for putting the crayons and paper
on my high chair tray all those years ago.

KATE

Table of Contents

A Pennsylvania Pledge

Oh, Pennsylvania, how we praise thee!
Land where the Quakers came to be free.
Independence for all was your decree
when your famous bell rang for Liberty.

Oh, Pennsylvania, as far as the eye can see,
endless mountains crowned with the hemlock tree
and rich valleys filled with our nation's history.
Oh, Pennsylvania, you are the place for me.

Our Nation's Keystone

Pennsylvania is nicknamed the Keystone State. A keystone is the last stone placed by the stonemason at the top of an arch. It holds the two sides of the archway together, keeping it strong and stable.

Along the Atlantic Coast the 13 original colonies form an arch, too. If you turn a map of the colonies sideways, you can see that Pennsylvania is in the center of that arch, just like the keystone of a stone archway. Our young nation was born in Philadelphia, and Pennsylvania held the northern and southern colonies together as they fought for independence, becoming the United States.

Many key battles in the Revolutionary and Civil Wars took place in Pennsylvania.

After the Civil War, Pennsylvania's natural resources, coal, steel, and oil, were key in rebuilding our nation, again keeping it strong.

Pennsylvania has earned its nickname, the Keystone State.

Hidden Symbols of Pennsylvania

Hidden in this picture are 12 symbols of Pennsylvania.
How many can you find?

The Liberty Bell / The Betsy Ross Flag / An Amish Straw Hat
The State Dog (*A Great Dane*) / The State Animal (*A Deer*) / A Quill Pen
The State Tree (*A Hemlock Pine Tree*) / A Three Corner Hat
We the People (*First words of the Constitution*) / A Pretzel
Benjamin Franklin / The State Flower (*The Mountain Laurel*)

5

The Story of Penn's Woods

Long ago, in the year 1682, a ship named *Welcome* sailed up the Delaware River. Onboard was an English Quaker named William Penn. Many Quaker families had sailed with him. They were happy to see the green wooded land that would be their new home.

One year before, in 1681, King Charles II had granted William Penn 45,000 square miles east of the Delaware River to repay a debt he owed Admiral Sir Penn, William's father. He made William Penn the governor of this new colony to rule as he wished.

William Penn wanted to name his new colony Sylvania, which means "woods." But the king thought it should be named to honor Admiral Sir Penn. So William agreed and his new colony became known as Pennsylvania, which means "Penn's Woods."

The king also wanted to rid England of the Quakers, which he called troublemakers. Not only could he get rid of his debt, but he could send the Quakers to this vast forest in North America where they would never be heard from again. The king thought he was very smart indeed.

But William Penn was smarter. He had a vision of Pennsylvania as a place of religious freedom and independence, where people had the right to govern themselves.

Even before his arrival, William Penn designed a new city between the Delaware and Schuylkill Rivers, with wide streets, open parks, a central market, and a public square. He named it Philadelphia, a Greek word meaning "The City of Brotherly Love." He dreamed it would be the center of his new plan called the "Holy Experiment."

Next, he established a General Assembly which passed the Great Law, giving people the right to life, liberty, religious freedom, and land ownership. William Penn had planted the seeds of the Declaration of Independence and the United States Constitution.

From deep within the mighty forests, majestic mountains, and lush green valleys of Penn's Woods was born a new idea, a new way of living that would become the United States of America. William Penn's dream had come true.

Seasons on an Amish Farm

Spring

Wake up, sleepyhead, Spring is here,
with fields to plow and sheep to shear.

Time to rake the new mown hay,
and watch spring lambs romp and play.

Quick, let's plant the garden patch,
before the chicks all do hatch.

Summer

Rise up early on a Summer's day,
to milk the cows and stack the hay.

Then berries to pick and gardens to weed,
eggs to gather and chickens to feed.

Time for a picnic by the old shade tree,
then busy, busy as a honeybee.

Fall

Fall is here, let's harvest the crop,
gather in firewood, *chop, chop, chop.*

Apples piled high till the cellar's full,
then knit a scarf from our sheep's wool.

Don't forget squash and pumpkins to pick,
now time to share a tasty drumstick.

Winter

Winter has come, the fields are white,
let's stitch a quilt for this cozy night.

And grind some corn into cornmeal,
mend the harness and fix a wheel.

Hitch up old Nan for a winter sleigh ride,
then over the snow we'll swiftly glide.

Colorful Riddles

I am black with a bright orange triangle.
You can find me on country roads.
I am usually hitched to a horse.
What am I?

I am red, white, and blue.
I have a circle and stripes and stars.
I first appeared in Philadelphia in 1776.
What am I?

I am gray and brown and furry
with black paws.
I have a very important shadow.
Men in top hats make a fuss over me on
February 2nd.
Who am I?

I am all colors.
I come in a green and yellow box.
Young artists love me.
What am I?

On Market Day

In Lancaster town
on Market Day,
10 shoofly pies sit
on display.

Big Billy Goat
stopped by to dine.
Now **8** shoofly pies
sit in a line.

Old Mother Hen
ordered two to go.
Now **6** shoofly pies
sit in a row.

Bessie Cow stopped by
to stuff herself.
Now **4** shoofly pies sit
on the shelf.

Along came a big dog,
in fact, a Great Dane.
Now **2** shoofly pies are
all that remain.

Then Mama's piglets squealed
Yummy, Yum, Yum!
And not a shoofly pie was left,
not even a crumb!

The baker took a look and saw
there were none.
"Oh no!" cried the baker,
"Market Day has just begun!"

Quickly that baker did
measure, mix, and pour.
And just in the nick of time,
he'd baked **10** more!

A Funny Word for a Fancy Bird

What in the world is a distelfink?
Is it brown, purple, red, black, blue, or pink?
Is it related to the long-lost missing link?
Does it give off a terrible, horrible stink?
What do you think is a distelfink?

The distelfink is a symbol of the Pennsylvania Dutch. This fanciful bird is widely seen in Pennsylvania Dutch country and is used to decorate many handcrafted items. It resembles a very colorful goldfinch, painted with red, yellow, black, white, and blue.

The old story goes that when God was creating the birds, the distelfink was the last to be painted, so God used all the leftover paint. That is why it is so fancy and colorful.

Daniel Boone
A Pennsylvania Boyhood

Daniel Boone was born in a Berks County log cabin in 1734, the sixth child in a Quaker family with eleven children.

Daniel would rather explore the great outdoors than go to school. His father's farm was on the edge of the frontier so he learned about the plants, trees, and animals that lived in the surrounding wilderness. Back in the mountains north of the Boone homestead, the Delaware Indians still lived in the nearby valleys. The Boone family befriended their Native American neighbors and Daniel learned their ways. He could track any animal, hide his own tracks, and even track the Delaware, too.

When Daniel was 10 years old, Squire Boone bought a large pasture for his cattle; but it was four miles from the homestead, so Daniel was sent to watch the herd. A year or two later, Squire Boone gave Daniel his first gun, a short rifle. But instead of watching the herd, Daniel went hunting. When he didn't return his worried family sent out a search party. After several frantic days searching for the missing boy, they spotted smoke rising from a back-country valley. There was Daniel, safe and contented, with fresh meat roasting on a fire and nearby a cozy shelter he'd built himself. The fearless young woodsman was right at home.

By the time Daniel was 15, he knew every animal trail, Indian path, mountaintop, and nearby valley like the back of his hand. That year Squire Boone decided the area was getting too settled, so he moved the family to the mountains of North Carolina.

Daniel Boone became a famous explorer and frontiersman. He discovered the Cumberland Gap which gave settlers a way to cross the Appalachian Mountains and settle Kentucky. But it was his early boyhood years in Pennsylvania that taught him the skills that he needed and used throughout his long life.

Betsy Ross
A Pennsylvania Girlhood

Her name was Elizabeth Griscom, but everyone called her Betsy. Born on January 1, 1752, Betsy was the eighth child in a large Quaker family.

Betsy dressed plainly in a gray dress, white apron, and cap as most Quaker children did in Philadelphia. She attended Friends Public School with her brothers and sisters eight hours a day, six days a week. Then there were all the chores. Yet Betsy managed to find time to do what she loved most, sewing with Great Aunt Sarah.

Great Aunt Sarah, who lived with the Griscom family, was an expert seamstress and had owned her own sewing business, something quite unusual in colonial times. She and Betsy shared a natural talent and love of sewing. Aunt Sarah taught Betsy to sew, often making her rip out stitches and do them over and over until she got them right. But Betsy didn't mind. She was learning how to be strong and independent like her great aunt, two traits that would last Betsy her lifetime. As more Griscom children were born, 17 in all, Betsy and Great Aunt Sarah kept busy making baby clothes.

By age 12, Betsy had finished her schooling so her father arranged an apprenticeship at Webster's Upholstery Shop so she could learn a trade. Betsy was not paid, but she learned how to make slipcovers, drapes, bedding, to upholster chairs and run a business. She also met John Ross, an apprentice her own age. In time the two married and opened their own upholstery shop on Arch Street.

In May of 1776, it is believed that George Washington asked Betsy Ross to sew a new national flag. By now Betsy was an expert needlewoman with a good eye for design. She changed the shape from a square to a rectangle, then added five-pointed stars. Washington was pleased and on June 14, 1777, the Second Continental Congress made it the official flag of the United States. But it will always be known as the Betsy Ross flag. Great Aunt Sarah would have been proud.

Country Quilting Party

When softly falls the snow,
and Mother makes bread dough,
time to snip, stitch, and sew,
gathered by our window.

Back-and-forth, to-and-fro,
three neat squares in a row,
some are red and indigo,
now our quilt starts to grow.

Stop by and say hello,
play a game of tic-tac-toe,
mark an X, mark an O,
3 times 3 is 9, you know.

Snip and trim, stitch and sew,
nine patch squares of calico,
each square tied with a bow,
watch our quilt quickly grow.

Outside the snow doth blow,
but we smell baking dough,
as we snip, stitch, and sew,
one snug day long ago.

The World's Largest Deposit of Coal

Coal has always been one of Pennsylvania's most valuable natural resources. Hard coal is called anthracite. Beneath Pennsylvania's mountains lies the largest deposit of hard coal in the world.

About 300 million years ago Pennsylvania was covered with a dense rain forest and vast swampland. It was called the *Carboniferous* period. During this period mammoth animals roamed the land. As the rain forest and huge animals died out, their remains were compressed over eons of time into huge underground deposits of hard coal covering 484 square miles.

Hard coal was first discovered in the late 1700s. According to one story a hunter in Schuylkill County was tired and cold, so he sought shelter under a rock ledge. He built a fire to warm himself but soon felt heat pouring down on his head. When he looked up, the rock ledge was glowing with warmth because it was actually made of hard coal that was starting to burn.

Soon, hard coal became a very valuable source of energy. Tons of coal were transported by wagon, canal boat, and railway to fuel our nation's industry. Home heating and cooking used coal, too. But mining coal was very dangerous work. The miners faced cave-ins, explosions, flooding, and coal dust, which eventually caused "black lung" disease. Yet the demand for coal grew.

Over 10 billion tons of hard coal have been mined from Pennsylvania's rich anthracite fields, yet it still remains the world's largest deposit of coal.

vocabulary: premium / tiller
packet boat / helm

Franklin, the Lucky Mule

CHAPTER ONE

Along the Towpath

Back in 1840, Hank and Annie lived on a canal boat with their pa, ma, and baby sister Ruthie. Pa was a good boatman who worked hard. His barge carried coal from mines in the mountains down to the big city of Philadelphia. Ma worked hard, too. She cooked on an old stove, did laundry on the back deck, and hung their clothes on the railings to dry. The children played on the flat roof of the cabin. This kept them safely out of the way when Pa was working the boat.

All along the towpath were mule stations where Pa would stop and exchange the mules that pulled the boat along the canals. Then Ma would pick up fresh supplies while Hank and Annie played on the grassy banks of the canal. Sometimes they would meet and play games with other canal boat children until Pa called, "Hurry on board now. Time's a' wasting." Then Hank and Annie would rush across the plank, waving goodbye as their boat home floated down the canal.

CHAPTER TWO
Everyone's Favorite Mule

Franklin was their favorite mule. He was strong and always willing to pull hard.

"Franklin knows the route as well as I do," said Pa. "We always make good time with Franklin."

"And he brays a loud warning when there is a low bridge ahead," said Ma gratefully. "I never have to worry about the children getting knocked off the boat."

"And Franklin is the only mule who lets me ride him," added Hank.

"And he lets me braid wildflowers in his

tail and mane," beamed Annie.

On hot summer days, Hank let Franklin wear his straw hat while Annie picked sweet clover for him to eat. Yes, Franklin was everyone's favorite mule.

"It's our lucky day when we get Franklin," smiled Pa.

CHAPTER THREE
Cold Snap

That fall there was a severe cold snap. Folks in Philadelphia began to run out of coal and the price shot up. The coal merchants decided to pay a premium for each ton of coal to reach the city during the cold snap. Word spread up the canal like wildfire. The race was on.

Overloaded coal barges started moving as fast as they could. This overworked the mules and they became exhausted. But these greedy boatmen pushed the mules anyway. Many got sick.

Pa wanted to win the extra money, too. Ma needed a new cookstove and the boat needed repairs. But Pa wasn't a greedy man.

"An overloaded barge is hard to steer," said Pa. "I'll take my usual load, Jake," he told the coal loader. "I'll not put my family in danger."

But when Pa stopped for a mule, the stable manager said he was too late.

"Most boatmen have taken two and three mules," said the stable manager. "I only have one mule left, Franklin."

"Franklin!" exclaimed Pa happily. "I'll take him."

But when they saw Franklin they knew something was terribly wrong. His head hung low, his ears flopped down, and he had a nasty cough.

"Someone worked him hard," said the stable manager. "You don't have to take him."

Pa was angry. "I said I'd take him, and I will."

Hank and Annie ran to Franklin. "How could anyone do this to Franklin?" they cried.

Ma hoisted baby Ruthie on her hip and

looked doubtful. "It's not going to be our lucky day," she sighed.

Franklin stumbled over to the harness at the end of the towline, always willing to go to work, but Pa said, "No work for you, old fella. Today you're going to ride."

Pa led Franklin up the ramp and put him on the canal boat. Then Pa harnessed himself to the towline and began to pull. Jake pushed the boat out into the canal with a long pole, and very slowly, they inched down the canal.

Hank covered Franklin with a blanket. Annie warmed some milk. Ma baked fresh cornbread and poured on some molasses. "Here, Franklin," she said. "This will set you right."

Chapter Four
Bad Luck Turns to Good Luck

Many canal boats passed by that day. The odd sight of Franklin riding and Pa pulling made people point and laugh. "Get a horse!" one boatman hooted. But Pa just kept on plodding along.

Later, a fancy packet boat filled with passengers bound for Philadelphia glided by. Everyone gawked until someone yelled "Which one's the dumb mule?" and they all laughed. Pa didn't pay any attention.

When Hank wasn't helping Pa pull the boat, he gave Franklin a warm rubdown. Ma kept feeding Franklin cornbread and molasses while Annie kept the warm milk coming. Just then a weak bray came from Franklin. Ma looked up and sure enough, there was a low bridge ahead. "I think Franklin is starting to mend," Ma called out to Pa.

The next day they passed an overloaded canal boat that had run into a bridge and

another one that had sunk. Pa just kept his head down and pulled.

Then something amazing happened. While Ma and Annie were busy with baby Ruthie, and Hank and Pa had their heads down pulling along the towpath, no one saw the big fallen tree in the water dead ahead. But Franklin saw it. He leaned into the tiller and steered the boat around the tree. Pa looked up just in time to flip the towline over the branches so it didn't tangle. Then he looked at Franklin standing proudly at the helm, keeping the boat on course.

"Whew, Franklin just saved us from disaster," said Pa. "It turned out to be our lucky day after all!"

CHAPTER FIVE
One Lucky Mule

The next day Franklin was feeling better. He took a turn at pulling the boat and they made up some lost time. But Pa didn't overwork him. He made Franklin ride in the boat every so often while Hank gave him a rubdown. Soon Franklin pulled all day long, and they began to pass other coal barges.

Then Philadelphia came into sight. There were other coal barges ahead of them, but they weren't last in line, thanks to Franklin. Pa was paid extra money for his load of coal. With some of the money, he bought Franklin the best hay he could find.

As Franklin happily munched on the sweet hay Pa put his arm around him. "It was our lucky day when we got you, Franklin," he said.

And it was Franklin's lucky day, too.

Pennsylvania's Water Highways

Pennsylvania is the only Middle Atlantic state that does not touch the Atlantic Ocean. But it is not landlocked. Its five major rivers and Great Lakes port make it accessible to any place in the world.

Because Pennsylvania has high mountains and steep valleys that are heavily wooded, overland travel was nearly impossible for its early settlers. So its rivers became major travel routes and superhighways for prosperous trade.

The Delaware River is the eastern border of Pennsylvania. Philadelphia is located where the Schuylkill River enters the Delaware, creating the world's largest freshwater port. From here ships can travel to the Atlantic Ocean through the Delaware Bay.

The Susquehanna River flows south through the central part of the state. This scenic meandering river, named after the Susquehannak people, reaches all the way to the Chesapeake Bay and the Atlantic Ocean, too.

In western Pennsylvania, the Allegheny and the Monongahela Rivers are the largest rivers in the state. They join at Pittsburgh to form the mighty Ohio River. From Pittsburgh, cargo can be shipped to the west and south by way of the Mississippi River and the Gulf of Mexico. This makes Pittsburgh one of the busiest inland ports in the United States.

In the northwestern section of the state, the lake port of Erie, on Lake Erie, gives Pennsylvania access to the Great Lakes, the Upper Midwest, and the St. Lawrence Seaway.

These navigable water highways have played a major role in making Pennsylvania a prosperous state throughout its history.

Letters Across the
Mason-Dixon Line

When the colonies of Maryland and Pennsylvania got into a dispute over their borders, they hired two surveyors, Charles Mason and Jeremiah Dixon, to settle the argument. In 1763 Mason and Dixon began mapping out the exact borderline, marking it with large stones. The job took four years and became known as the Mason-Dixon Line. Nearly 100 years later during the Civil War, it became the dividing line between the North and the South.

In 1863 the Mason-Dixon Line also separated two young girl cousins, Phebe McAllister and Annabelle Thompson. Living just a Sunday's buggy ride apart, they had always been close and spent weeks together each summer. Here are their letters.

Emmitsburg, Maryland
June 18, 1863
My Dear Cousin Phebe,

I bear the saddest of news. Ma forbids me to visit you this summer, now that the war is at our doorstep. Her people come from Old Virginia and she vows no daughter of hers will set foot north of the Mason-Dixon Line. Elijah, along with Cousin Oscar, has enlisted in the Confederate Army. They are quartered near Winchester. Elijah's letters say they will be shipped north soon which puts Ma in a stew. Lately Union soldiers have been passing our farm in large numbers which only adds to Ma's fretting. She won't even let me give them our sweet well water.

Oh my dear Phebe, it is unthinkable that we shall not spend our summer days together as we always have. I so longed to go berry picking on that pretty ridge in back of your farm. Did you finish your pretty blue print sunbonnet? Remember, we were supposed to wear them berry picking this summer? I started the ruffle on mine, but Ma has me knitting socks for Elijah.

I remain your devoted cousin and dearest friend,
Annabelle

Gettysburg, Pennsylvania
June 27, 1863
My Dear Cousin Annabelle,

I am greatly saddened by your news along with everything else this summer. Rumors are running rampant in Gettysburg that the Confederates are marching from Chambersburg, taking everything they can get their hands on. Many folks are packing up and fleeing north to safety. The road by our farm is choked with loaded wagons. Pa says he won't leave the farm, not while one brick is still standing. Our Henry has gone, too, as have the neighbor boys, Jonah and Pubrick. Remember last summer how they chased us with that snake? Oh how we did squeal. Now they are chasing your boys in gray with guns.

My dear Annabelle, promise me we will stay united even if our country is divided.

Your dear cousin who misses you,
Phebe

Emmitsburg, Maryland
July 8, 1863
My Dearest Phebe,

You have my solemn promise, my dear cousin. Nothing
will separate us, except what I am about to tell you.
Ma and I are leaving for Winchester, Virginia, to live
with Grandma Merriweather. Ma wants to help in the
hospital there and keep an eye out for Elijah and Oscar.
Pa is staying here with little Willy to protect the farm.
Ma thinks we will be safer in the South with her people,
but after Gettysburg, the reports aren't good. We have
heard it was a terrible battle up there. I pray that you
were far removed from the action and are unharmed.

Your affectionate cousin and dearest friend forever,
Annabelle

PS: I managed to finish my blue calico bonnet in
spite of everything.

Gettysburg, Pennsylvania
July 11, 1863
My Cherished Cousin Annabelle,

We have had a most terrible battle here and have
spent days hiding in our cellar. Our windows and
shutters were shot to pieces but we remain unharmed.
When we emerged, there were many wounded soldiers
in our yard and barn. We have opened our house to
them and are caring for as many as possible. One
is a Confederate, and I am caring for him as though
he were your dear brother Elijah. Ma says as soon
as possible he will be shipped north to a Union
prison hospital in Mechanicsburg, but we are keeping him as long as possible for he is most polite
and appreciative of our kindness.

Your solemn promise that nothing will separate us
has given me heart. Let us make one more promise.
When this war is over, let us wear our blue bonnets

and meet by that old stone north of your farm which is one of the markers of the Mason-Dixon Line. We shall dance for joy on that day with no line between us forevermore.

I remain your loyal cousin and dearest friend forever,
Phebe

Lincoln's Gettysburg Address

On November 19, 1863, just four months after the Battle of Gettysburg, President Abraham Lincoln traveled by train to Gettysburg to dedicate the National Cemetery. The platform on Cemetery Hill was crowded with many dignitaries. The ceremony was long. Edward Everett was the main speaker. His speech lasted for two hours. Finally President Lincoln was introduced. The tall thin melancholy man in the black suit and top hat spoke to the crowd of over 15,000 in a strong voice.

But Lincoln's speech lasted just two minutes. Its ten sentences contained less than 300 simple words. Some say Lincoln's brief writing style was self taught, because as a

poor frontier boy, he had to practice writing with charcoal on the back of a farm shovel. Yet these simple words, written and delivered by President Lincoln to a nation torn by the Civil War, deeply expressed what is uniquely American, and became one of our most significant documents.

From the state of Pennsylvania, birthplace of the Declaration of Independence and the United States Constitution, came our third greatest document, the Gettysburg Address.

The Gettysburg Address

"Fourscore and seven years ago our fathers brought forth on this continent a new nation, conceived in liberty, and dedicated to the proposition that all men are created equal.

Now we are engaged in a great civil war, testing whether that nation, or any nation so conceived and so dedicated, can long endure. We are met on a great battlefield of that war. We have come to dedicate a portion of that field as a final resting-place for those who here gave their lives that this nation might live. It is altogether fitting and proper that we should do this.

But in a larger sense, we cannot dedicate—we cannot consecrate—we cannot hallow this ground. The brave men, living and dead, who struggled here, have consecrated it far above our poor power to add or detract.

The world will little note nor long remember what we say here, but it can never forget what they did here. It is for us, the living, rather, to be dedicated here to the unfinished work which they who fought here have thus far so nobly advanced. It is rather for us to be here dedicated to the great task remaining before us—that from these honored dead we take increased devotion to that cause for which they gave the last full measure of devotion; that we here highly resolve that these dead shall not have died in vain; that this nation, under God, shall have a new birth of freedom; and that government of the people, by the people, for the people shall not perish from the earth."

November 19, 1863

The Mountain Laurel

When clusters of pink blossoms appear,
carpeting every hill, glen, and slope,
Mountain Laurel arrives with bright cheer,
announcing springtime's promise and hope.

Its delicate beauty has no peer,
yet sturdy with dense green bower,
providing a safe thicket for deer,
Mountain Laurel is our state flower.

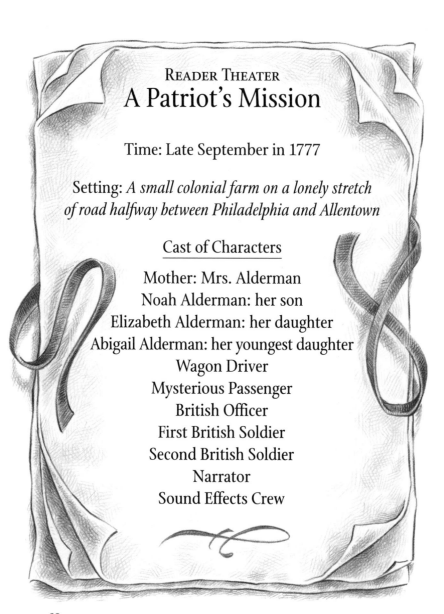

READER THEATER
A Patriot's Mission

Time: Late September in 1777

Setting: *A small colonial farm on a lonely stretch of road halfway between Philadelphia and Allentown*

Cast of Characters

Mother: Mrs. Alderman
Noah Alderman: her son
Elizabeth Alderman: her daughter
Abigail Alderman: her youngest daughter
Wagon Driver
Mysterious Passenger
British Officer
First British Soldier
Second British Soldier
Narrator
Sound Effects Crew

ACT ONE
Scene One: The Aldermans' Small Farmhouse

Narrator: *It is early morning on the Alderman farm. Outside, a rooster crows. Mother is serving hot porridge from a black kettle hanging over a crackling fire in her humble home. Noah and Elizabeth are seated at the table, having a lively discussion. Young Abigail is trying to follow every word of her older brother and sister.*

Noah: (*bangs fist on table*) I am so a Patriot! And I don't care who knows it!

Elizabeth: (*using the voice of reason*) But Noah, it's dangerous to be a Patriot these days!

Noah: (*clenches fist*) I'm not afraid of the British! Just let them set a toe on our farm and I'll show them!

Abigail: (*in her small voice*) If Noah's a Parrot then I'm a Parrot! Bethie, don't you want to be a Parrot, too?

Noah: (*snickers, pokes Elizabeth's shoulder and makes chicken sounds*) Or maybe Bethie wants to be a chicken.

Elizabeth: (*shrugs shoulders, ignores Noah, and speaks in a patient voice*) Abby, it's not a Parrot. It's a Patriot. It means that you are loyal to our new nation and support Washington's army which is fighting for independence from Great Britain. If you are a Loyalist, that means you want British rule and don't want to be independent.

Noah: (*still teasing Elizabeth*) Or it means you are a chicken ... cluck, cluck, cluck ...

Mother: Children, hush! Stop your squabbling! It's hard enough to run this farm without your father. Now eat your porridge before it gets cold. There is much work to be done today.

Narrator: *At the mention of their father the children grow silent and quietly eat their porridge. Noah is first to break the silence.*

Noah: (*speaking seriously now*) It's been a long time since we've heard from Father, hasn't it, Mother?

Mother: (*sits down wearily and sighs*) Yes, it has. In his last letter he was guarding a powder depot near Philadelphia. But now the British have surrounded Philadelphia and will soon march in and take over the city. I've heard that bands of British redcoats are scouring the country-side, foraging for food. Your Aunt Ruth said a pig is missing from their farm down in Pottstown.

Elizabeth: Mother, do you think they will come out this far?

Mother: Well, just in case, I'm moving the pigs and chickens into the barn today. And the straw in the far meadow must be raked and stacked today, too, plus all the apples must be picked soon or they will spoil. (*sighs again*) I don't know how I can manage it all. (*Mother covers her face with her apron, hiding her worry as the children gather around her.*)

Elizabeth: (*pouring a cup of tea for her mother*) Mother, you are exhausted. Noah and I can stack the straw in the far meadow today.

Noah: Yes, Mother. Father showed me how to do it properly.

Elizabeth: And we'll take Abby with us so you can rest a while.

Abby: I may be small, but I can help, too, Mother.

Mother: (*wiping a tear with the corner of her apron*) I am so blessed to have such good children.

Scene Two: The Far Meadow

Narrator: *The three Alderman children have worked hard all day, but now the sun is setting. Crows call to each other as they roost in the nearby trees. It will be dark soon.*

Noah: Quick, let's finish this big stack before it gets dark.

Elizabeth: And let's make it extra big to please Mother.

Narrator: *Just as the children are finishing the big stack of straw they hear a wagon approaching, creaking under a very heavy load. The two strangers driving the wagon wear their coat collars up, scarves over their mouths, and hats set low. The wagon driver and his passenger pull up alongside the children.*

Wagon Driver: Good day, lad. Mind if I rest my horses a spell in your meadow? They're mighty tired.

Noah: Mind telling me what's in your wagon first?

Elizabeth: Noah, that's not very polite. Father would let them rest.

Mysterious Passenger: (*chuckles softly behind his scarf but remains silent*)

Wagon Driver: As you can see, lad, just sacks of flour.

Noah: (*looks skeptical but answers politely*) My sister is right, good sir. Please, rest your horses here as long as you like.

Narrator: *Just then the sound of marching soldiers is heard coming along the road. It is a British patrol. The wagon driver and his passenger frantically begin to cover the wagon with straw.*

Wagon Driver: Quick, children! Help us cover the wagon so the redcoats don't see it.

Noah: (*in an uncertain voice*) So they won't steal the sacks of flour?

Wagon Driver: Ah, right. We want them to think it's just a wagon of straw. Now stand in front of the wagon like everything is normal. We'll be hiding underneath. Sir, quick. Don't let them see you!

Mysterious Passenger: (*whispers with muffled voice from below the wagon*) For the Patriots, my son.

Narrator: *Noah and Elizabeth look puzzled but there is something in that muffled voice that makes the children trust the wagon driver and his passenger. As the British patrol approaches, Noah and Elizabeth cleverly pretend they are having a straw fight with Abigail.*

British Officer: Children, children! In the name of the King, what is going on here?

Elizabeth: (*innocently picking bits of straw from Abby's hair*) Just a bit of sport, sir.

Noah: Aye, sir, just a little fun after our hard day's work.

First Soldier: (*speaking aside to Second Soldier*) Just like these colonists, sending children to do a man's work. They'll never win this war. Not a chance.

Second Soldier: Right you are! Half that straw will fall off before that wagon reaches the barn. Shall we set it right for them, sir?

British Officer: Quiet, gentlemen! There isn't time. We must rendezvous with our company at Saunders' Grist Mill before dark. Could you children kindly direct us?

Elizabeth: Oh yes, sir. (*still using her innocent voice and pointing east*) It's about two miles that a'way.

Noah: (*with a little smile*) Aye, sir. You can't miss it.

Narrator: *The British Officer tips his hat to the children and the patrol heads off the wrong way because Elizabeth had cleverly pointed in the opposite direction of the mill. Noah smiles proudly at his sister.*

Noah: Oh, Beth, you are a Patriot after all!

Wagon Driver: (*crawling out from under the wagon*) She certainly is. You all are! And I thank you kindly. Now you'd best be getting home before it gets any darker. We'll just rest here for the night and be off at first light.

Narrator: *As the Alderman children walk toward their farmhouse, a large moon begins to rise. Noah glances back and sees the mysterious passenger strangely watching them until they reach the edge of the yard.*

Act Two
Scene One: Later that Night in the Farmhouse

Narrator: *It is nearly midnight at the Aldermans' farmhouse. The moon has risen high overhead as owls hoot from the woods. Mrs. Alderman, overly tired from her hard work, sleeps soundly but Noah is awake. There are many questions on his mind. Why did the wagon driver address his passenger as "Sir"? And why did the passenger watch them walk home? What was it about his voice? Plus, that wagon was loaded down with something much heavier than sacks of flour. Something is amiss and Noah is determined to find out what it is. He dresses quickly and tiptoes into his sisters' room.*

Noah: (*in a loud whisper*) Beth, Beth. Wake up. I'm going to the far meadow. I want to see what is really in that wagon. I think they are hiding something, and I'm going to find out what it is.

Elizabeth: (*rubbing sleep from her eyes*) You're not going without me. I want to see it, too. And there was something about that passenger.

Abigail: (*popping out of bed*) Me, too! I want to go, too.

Noah: All right. Now get on your capes and not a peep out of either of you till we get outside. We don't want to wake Mother.

Scene Two: After Midnight in the Far Meadow

Narrator: *The Alderman children take the path to the far meadow. Again, owls hoot from the woods. Mice rustle in the leaves. A possum's eyes glow in the moonlight. Abigail shivers with fright and hangs onto Elizabeth's cape as Noah leads the way. Suddenly, a soldier steps in front of them with a musket. All three children stop with a gasp.*

Soldier: Halt! Who goes there! Friend or foe?

Noah: Ah, don't you mean Patriot or Loyalist?

Elizabeth: No Loyalists here.

Abigail: Right! We're all Parrots here!

Soldier: (*starts to laugh*) Parrots? Is that my little Abby?

Abigail: Father?

Noah and Elizabeth and Abigail: (*running forward*) Father! Oh, Father! It is you!

Father: I'm sorry, my dear children. I couldn't reveal myself to you this afternoon. It was too dangerous.

Noah: Father, are you on a secret mission?

Father: Yes, Son. Come, let me show you what is in the wagon. It will explain everything.

Narrator: *The wagon driver stirs from his bed of straw as the children help their father, Lieutenant Alderman, remove the straw and sacks of flour. The bright moonlight reveals something massive and shiny. The children take a step backward in awe.*

Noah: Father, what is it?

Lt. Alderman: It is Pennsylvania's state bell. It rang when our new nation was born in Philadelphia, when we declared independence last year on July 4th.

Elizabeth: Father, were you there?

Lt. Alderman: Yes. I heard the first reading of the Declaration of Independence, and then this magnificent bell rang loud and clear for liberty. I will never forget it. And that is why I volunteered for this secret mission, to hide this symbol of freedom from the British.

Elizabeth: Oh, Father, you are so brave.

Father: (*beaming with pride*) Not half as brave as my children.

Noah: (*eagerly*) Oh, Father, can I touch it?

Father: (*taking little Abby by the hand*) Come, I want all of you to touch it. It is your future.

Narrator: *On that moonlit night back in 1777, three small hands reached out and touched what would become known as the Liberty Bell, a symbol of freedom for the whole country. And in the days and weeks that followed that night, Lieutenant Alderman and the wagon driver secreted all the church bells out of Philadelphia, and the children helped hide the bells in straw stacks overnight before they were transported on to safety. And when the war was over, Lieutenant Alderman returned to his family and named his homestead Bell Meadow Farm.*

A Pennsylvania Timeline

Lenape Indians inhabit Pennsylvania.

1500s

New Sweden: First European settlement near present-day Philadelphia.

1638

1682

1685

William Penn arrives and lays out a new government.

Philadelphia (The City of Brotherly Love) becomes the capital of Pennsylvania.

1723

Ben Franklin arrives in Philadelphia.

1754

French and Indian War begins at Fort Necessity.

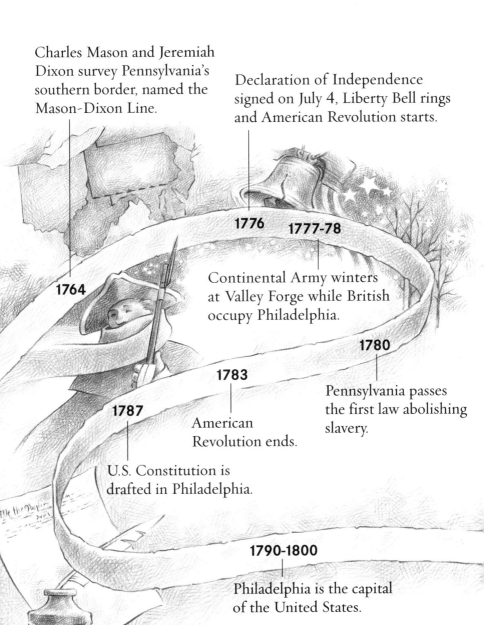

Charles Mason and Jeremiah Dixon survey Pennsylvania's southern border, named the Mason-Dixon Line.

Declaration of Independence signed on July 4, Liberty Bell rings and American Revolution starts.

1776

1777-78

1764

Continental Army winters at Valley Forge while British occupy Philadelphia.

1780

1783

Pennsylvania passes the first law abolishing slavery.

1787

American Revolution ends.

U.S. Constitution is drafted in Philadelphia.

1790-1800

Philadelphia is the capital of the United States.

85

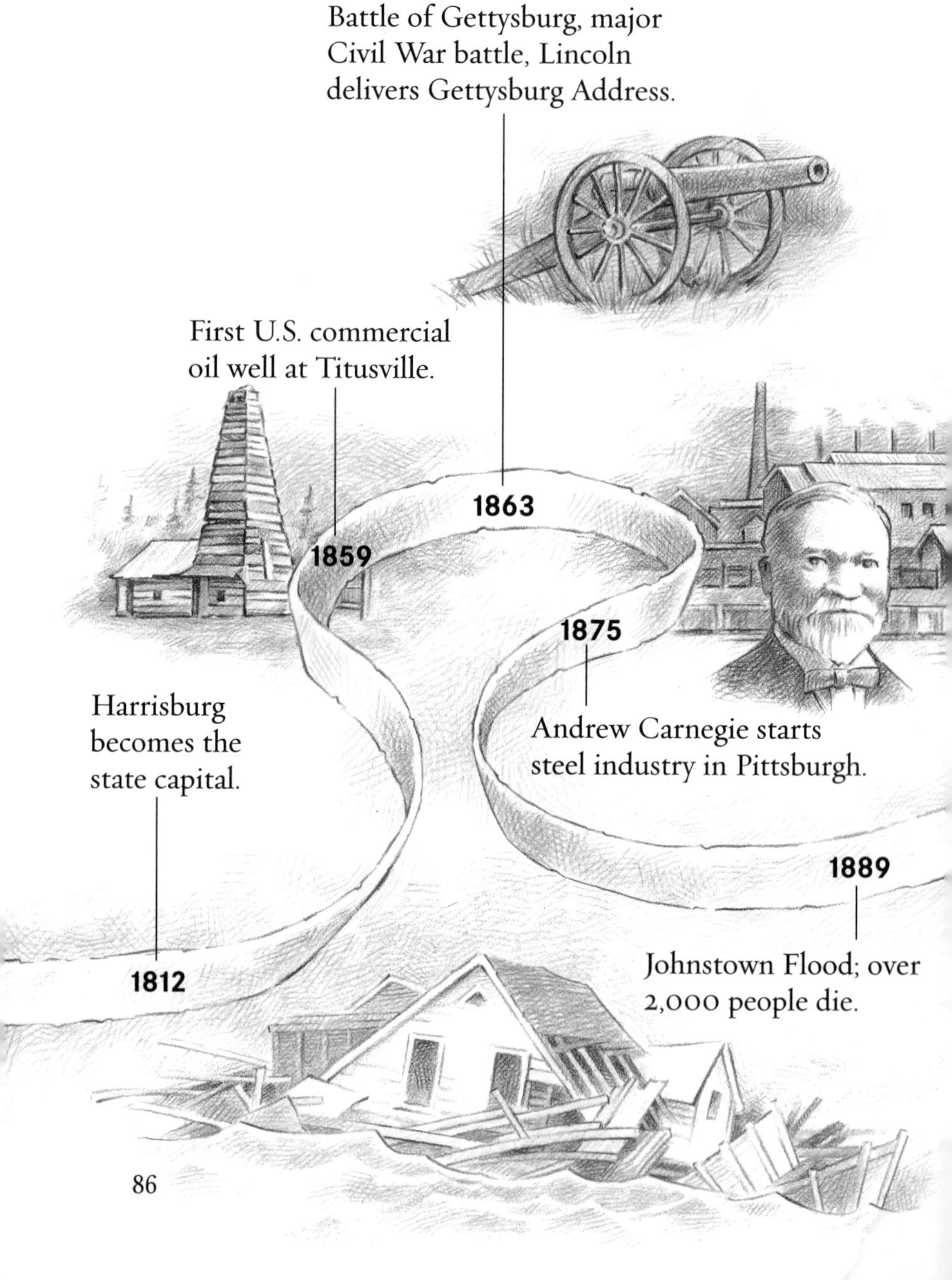

Battle of Gettysburg, major
Civil War battle, Lincoln
delivers Gettysburg Address.

First U.S. commercial
oil well at Titusville.

1863

1859

1875

Harrisburg
becomes the
state capital.

Andrew Carnegie starts
steel industry in Pittsburgh.

1889

1812

Johnstown Flood; over
2,000 people die.

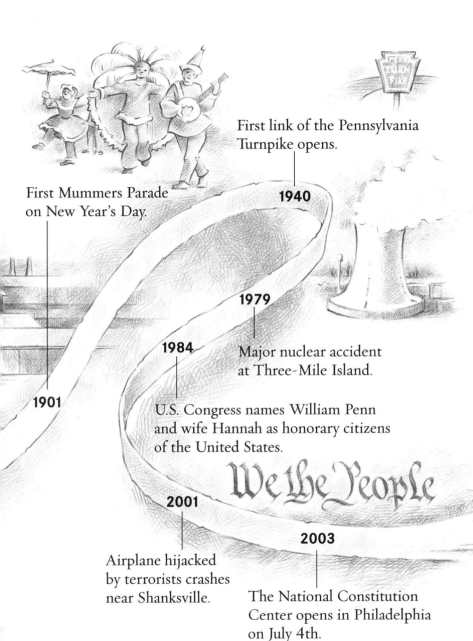

First link of the Pennsylvania Turnpike opens.

1940

First Mummers Parade on New Year's Day.

1979

1984

Major nuclear accident at Three-Mile Island.

1901

U.S. Congress names William Penn and wife Hannah as honorary citizens of the United States.

We the People

2001

2003

Airplane hijacked by terrorists crashes near Shanksville.

The National Constitution Center opens in Philadelphia on July 4th.

Be Proud of Pennsylvania

Be proud of where you live.
Be brave and take a stand.
To try each day and give
your best to this good land.

Be proud and stand up tall.
Reach out with a helping hand.
Give brotherly love to all
in Pennsylvania, your homeland.

Trinka Hakes Noble

Trinka Hakes Noble is the award-winning author of numerous picture books including *The Scarlet Stockings Spy* (an IRA Teachers' Choice 2005), *The Last Brother*, and *The Legend of the Cape May Diamond*. Ms. Noble also wrote the ever-popular *Jimmy's Boa* series and *Meanwhile Back at the Ranch*, both featured on PBS's *Reading Rainbow*. Her many awards include ALA Notable Children's Book, *Booklist* Children's Editors' Choice, IRA-CBC Children's Choice, *Learning*: The Year's Ten Best, and several Junior Literary Guild selections.

Ms. Noble has studied children's book writing and illustrating in New York City at Parsons School of Design, the New School University, Caldecott medalist Uri Shulevitz's Greenwich Village Workshop, and at New York University. A member of the Rutgers University Council on Children's Literature, she was awarded Outstanding Woman 2002 in Arts and Letters in the state of New Jersey for her lifetime work in children's books. Ms. Noble lives in northern New Jersey. Learn more at www.trinkahakesnoble.com.

K. L. Darnell

K. L. Darnell has been drawing pictures for as long as she can remember. She earned her BFA studying drawing and painting at the University of Michigan School of Art and Design. *The Pennsylvania Reader* is Ms. Darnell's seventh children's book with Sleeping Bear Press. In addition to her work as an illustrator, she specializes in the beautiful art of calligraphy and is an instructor of art at Lansing Community College. Ms. Darnell lives and works in East Lansing, Michigan.